This book is dedicated to Shirley Fryer,
my dear friend, leader, visionary, Children's Pastor &
Founder & Director of Children of Destiny.

Shirley, your love & passion for Jesus & His heart for children has marked me forever. Your devotion to Jesus is real, your forgiveness & genuine love towards others tangible & your desire to see every child truly know Jesus is contagious.

May this message reach children across the world, for your eternal legacy,
as you watch from the great cloud of witnesses.
Thank you for seeing us all like Jesus does.
We miss you every single day.

Destined for Greatness - God's Plan for Every Child

Written by Mandy Furlong
Illustrated by Mike Sam
Copyright © 2025 RaisingRevivalists

All rights reserved. No part of this book may be reproduced in any manner whatsoever without prior written permission of the publisher.

English Standard Version (ESV Bible) is used for scripture references.

First Printing, 2025

Published by Raising Revivalists
www.raisingrevivalists.com.au
@raisingrevivalists

ISBN 978-1-7640087-0-9

This story was originally the lyrics to a song recorded by Children of Destiny. Available on Spotify & other streaming platforms

When I was born, God made me

"You knitted me together in my mother's womb"
Psalm 139:13

He had a plan, to set me free

"For I know the plans I have for you declares the Lord"
Jeremiah 29:11

His word tells me, what's wrong and right

"For His word is living and active, sharper than any two-edged sword"
Hebrews 4:12

And if I choose His ways,
His love will shine bright

"God's love has been poured into our hearts through the Holy Spirit"
Romans 5:5

I am destined for GREATNESS

"But thanks be to God, who gives us the victory through our Lord Jesus Christ"
1 Corinthians 15:57

That's God's plan for me

"To give you a future and a hope"
Jeremiah 29:11

I am destined for GREATNESS

"But thanks be to God, who gives us the victory through our Lord Jesus Christ"
1 Corinthians 15:57

Because God lives in me

"It is no longer I who live, but Christ who lives in me"
Galations 2:20

My destiny is in His hands

*"Lead me in your truth and teach me,
for you are the God of my salvation"*
Psalm 25:5

He chose me for His master plan

"For we know, brothers loved by God, that he has chosen you"
1 Thessalonians 1:4

He saved the world and set them free

"For God did not send his Son into the world to condemn the world, but in order that the world might be saved through him"
John 3:17

So they would know their destiny

"So you also must consider yourselves dead to sin and alive to God in Christ Jesus"
Romans 6:11

I am destined for GREATNESS

"But thanks be to God, who gives us the victory through our Lord Jesus Christ"
1 Corinthians 15:57

That's God's plan for me

"To give you a future and a hope"
Jeremiah 29:11

I am destined for GREATNESS

"But thanks be to God, who gives us the victory through our Lord Jesus Christ"
1 Corinthians 15:57

Because God lives in me!

"It is no longer I who live, but Christ who lives in me"
Galations 2:20

www.ingramcontent.com/pod-product-compliance
Lightning Source LLC
Chambersburg PA
CBHW061126170426
43209CB00014B/1683